NATIONAL GEOGRAPHIC KIDS™

Awesome aNiMals

NATIONAL GEOGRAPHIC

WASHINGTON, D.C.

Visit us online:
Kids: nationalgeographic.com/kids
Parents: nationalgeographic.com
Teachers: nationalgeographic.com/education
Librarians: ngchildrensbooks.org

ISBN: 978-1-4263-0754-6

Printed in China

10/PPS/1

ILLUSTRATION CREDITS

FRONT COVER: (dolphin) Craig Tuttle/Aurora/Getty Images; (frog), Michael Turco; (koala), Thorsten Milse/ Picture Press/Photolibrary; (cheetah), Winfried Wisniewski/Corbis

BACK COVER: (lion), Adam Jones/PhotoDisc Red/Getty Images; (turtle), Ron Masessa/iStockphoto.com; (penguin), Joel Simon/Digital Vision; (wolves), Klein-Hubert/www.kimballstock.com

TITLE PAGE: Karl Ammann/Getty Images

BOTTLENOSE DOLPHIN: 3, Kristian Sekulic/iStockphoto. com; 4, artwork by Jim Paillot; 5, Daniel McCoulloch/ Digital Vision

CHEETAH: 7, Gerry Ellis/Minden Pictures/NationalGeo-graphicStock.com; 8, artwork by Jim Paillot; 9, Winfried Wisniewski/Corbis

ELEPHANT: 11, Javarman/Shutterstock; 12, Igor Janicek/ Shutterstock; 12 (UFO), Nick Koudis/PhotoDisc/Getty Images; 12 (baby), Lianne Halling; 13, Karl Ammann/ Getty Images

GIANT PANDA: 15, Lisa & Mike Husar; 16, Mark Thiessen, NGP; 17, Lisa & Mike Husar

RED-EYED TREE FROG: 19, Sebastian Duda/Shutterstock; 20, Mark Thiessen, NGP; 21, Mark Kostich/iStockphoto.com

LION: 23, Periquet Stephanie/National Geographic My Shot; 24 (dancing lions), Cory Thoman/Shutterstock; 24 (globe), Shutterstock; 24 (portrait), R. Martens/ Shutterstock; 24 (zebras), Gerry Ellis/Digital Vision; 24 (lioness), EcoPrint/Shutterstock; 24 (cub roaring), Eric Isselée/Shutterstock; 24 (steak), Robyn Mackenzie/ Shutterstock; 24 (savanna), ostill/Shutterstock; 25, Adam Jones/PhotoDisc Red/Getty Images

SEA TURTLE: 27, Ron Masessa/iStockphoto.com; 28, Jeff Hunter/Getty Images; 28 (goldfish), Superstock; 28 (rose), Jonathan Halling; 29, Masa Ushioda/www .coolwaterphoto.com

WOLF: 31, Mark Hamblin/Oxford Scientific/Photolibrary; 32 (wolf cartoon), Kristijan Hranisavljevic/iStockphoto. com; 32 (forest), Pakhnyushcha/Shutterstock; 32, (wolf howling) Gerry Ellis/Digital Vision; 32 (cub), John Pitcher/ iStockphoto.com; 32 (portrait), Holly Kuchera /Shutter-stock; 32 (jaw), Geoffrey Kuchera/Shutterstock; 32 (asteroid), dezignor/Shutterstock; 32 (wolves walking), Andy Gehrig/iStockphoto.com; 33, Klein-Hubert/www. kimballstock.com

PENGUIN: 35, Keith Szafranski/iStockphoto.com; 36, artwork by Dan Sipple; 37, Joel Simon/Digital Vision

KOALA: 39, Alain Mafart-Renodier/Bios/Photolibrary; 40, artwork by Dan Sipple; 41, Mitsuaki Iwago/Minden Pictures/NationalGeographicStock.com

bottLeNose doLphiN

Friendly and intelligent, bottlenose dolphins are like the puppy dogs of the ocean. They have curved mouths that make them look like they are always smiling, and they can be trained to perform surprising tricks. These marine mammals are also athletic. They can jump 10 to 20 feet (3 to 6 m) into the air and swim at speeds of up to 18 miles (29 km) an hour.

Bottlenose dolphins live in saltwater areas all around the world—except in polar waters. They must surface to breathe, sometimes as often as two or three times a minute. Dolphins live alone, in small groups called pods, or even in gatherings of hundreds. They like to communicate by brushing flippers, flukes, and bodies while constantly chattering in whistles and clicks. These noises help dolphins find their way around using echolocation. The clicks bounce off nearby objects. Dolphins listen for the echoes and can tell the approximate distance of food, even other dolphins. Talk about a built-in sound system!

dIvE in

Help the bottlenose dolphin mother and baby swim to the family reunion. Only one path through the sea will let them join the big family get-together!

ANSWERS ON PAGE 43

finiSh

staRt

4

NATIONAL
GEOGRAPHIC

Bottlenose dolphins have saved humans from shark attacks.

Dolphins have taste buds, and som

Individual dolphins have signature whistles, like people have names.

Like humans, bottlenose dolph

e even have food preferences.

ns can recognize themselves in a mirror.

Some bottlenose dolphins scare fish onto the beach to eat them.

Bottlenose dolphins' beaks are usually 3 inches (8 cm) long.

CHeeTah

In the wild world of records, cheetahs have one awesome claim to fame. These cool cats are the sports cars of the savanna! They can go from 0-60 miles (0-96 km) an hour in only three seconds, making them 50 percent faster than all other land animals. Cheetahs' slim, flexible frame helps them reach speeds of more than 70 miles (113 km) an hour, and their long, flat tail helps them balance on sharp turns while chasing prey. Unlike their larger lion cousins, cheetahs cannot roar. They can, however, purr, hiss, whine, growl, and chirp. Female cheetahs are loners and use these noises to communicate with their cubs. Male cheetahs, usually brothers, often live and hunt together and communicate not only vocally but even by twitching their ears!

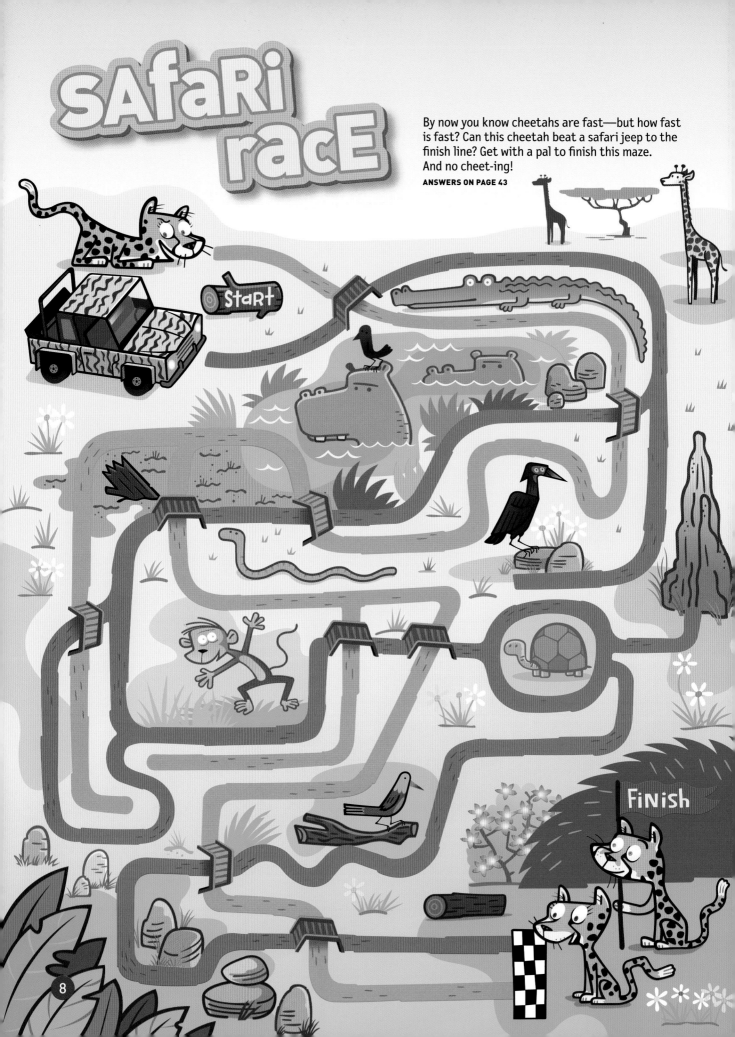

SAFaRi racE

By now you know cheetahs are fast—but how fast is fast? Can this cheetah beat a safari jeep to the finish line? Get with a pal to finish this maze. And no cheet-ing!

ANSWERS ON PAGE 43

Start

Finish

Cheetahs climb on tourist vehicles to look for prey.

Every cheetah paw is unique.

After a chase, a cheetah needs half an hour to catch its breath before it can eat.

The cheetah's tastiest prey is the Thomson's gazelle.

Ancient Egyptians kept cheetahs as pets.

NATIONAL
GEOGRAPHIC

eLephaNt

Imagine if you were over at a friend's house and your mom called you to come home. Not on the phone, but through the bottom of your feet. Crazy, right? Well for elephants—it's true! Elephants make many noises we can hear and even some we can't. Scientists believe these massive mammals make rumbling noises so low in frequency that the vibrations travel through the surface of the ground and tickle the toes of other elephants several miles away! This ability helps elephants communicate with family members, and strong family bonds are crucial to a herd's survival. Herds are made up of grandmothers, mothers, aunts, and calves. Males generally leave the herd when they become teenagers and live alone.

Double Take

See if you can spot 10 differences in the two pictures. **ANSWERS ON PAGE 43**

An elephant, a giraffe, and zebras visit a water hole in Africa.

12

h its trunk.   Elephants don't like the taste of chili powder.   Elephants can't jump.

aid of bees but not mice.   Elephants use their trunks as snorkels when they wade in deep water.

Elephants flap their large ears to stay cool.

An elephant can pick up a single blade of grass wi

Because of their size, adult elephants have no other enemies besides people.

Elephants are afr

giant PANda

If there was an animal eating contest, giant pandas just might take the cake! These black-and-white bears turn the bamboo forests of China where they live into an all-you-can-eat buffet! Bamboo isn't very nutritious, so pandas must spend up to 14 hours a day eating, but they're certainly built for it. Giant pandas have an elongated wrist bone that comes in handy when stripping stalks of bamboo. They use their sharp teeth to reach the soft tissue inside and their feet to help hold the long stalks up while they're chewing—that's why pandas usually eat sitting up!

Panda-monium!

Pandas may look like they stand out in a crowd, but believe it or not, in their snowy and rocky environment they're totally camouflaged. Take a look at the black-and-white objects below and see if you can find the following:

ANSWERS ON PAGE 43

6	soccer balls
4	pushpins
7	chess pieces
6	plastic utensils
5	clothespins
4	things you look through
3	number 8s
3	club cards
3	pandas
5	other animals

Like other bears, giant pandas like honey.

Pandas don't hunt, but they will eat meat.

The Chinese word for panda is *Daxiongmao,* which means "Great Bear-Cat."

They don't do it often, but pandas can swim!

The giant panda is one bear that doesn't hibernate in winter.

NATIONAL
GEOGRAPHIC

ReD-EYed TrEE fRog

Curled up in a tight little ball on a bright green leaf, this unassuming amphibian might go unnoticed. But once it opens its eyes and stretches out its arms and legs—that's a whole other story! The red-eyed tree frog lives in the rain forests of South America and spends its days hiding its brightly-marked body parts from possible predators. With glaring orange feet, blood-red eyes, and a striking blue and green body, these little guys stand out from their jungle-green surroundings. But their distinct look is actually a built-in defense strategy. When disturbed, they pop open their eyes and leap away, confusing enemies in a flash.

Slithery Slimy Search!

Uh oh! Someone freed all the snakes, frogs, lizards, and turtles in the reptile/amphibian exhibit at the zoo! See if you can find the following creepy crawlies to put them back where they belong:

ANSWERS ON PAGE 43

2	turtles
12	snakes
17	frogs
10	lizards

Not ready for the fun to end? Can you find these bonus items?

9	things that have yellow on them
4	things partly hidden under the leaves
4	gummy snakes
3	snakes sticking out their tongues
25	things with tails

to blend into their environment better.

is about the size of a teacup.

Females lay "clutches" of eggs on the underside of leaves.

Red-eyed tree frog embryos can hatch early to escape a snake!

NATIONAL
GEOGRAPHIC

Red-eyed tree frogs can change their body markings to a darker green or reddish brown to match their mood or

Males shake branches to mark their territory with vibrations.

The average red-eyed tree fro

Lion

If you ever hear someone call a lion "King of the Jungle," here's your opportunity to be a smarty pants. Tell them that "King of the Savanna" is more like it. Lions live in savanna, semi-desert, and plains in Africa and the open woodland Gir forest of Asia, but never in the jungle. Weighing up to 550 pounds (249 kg), lions are the second largest cat species in the world. Male lions are fierce protectors that patrol vast territories that generally span about 100 square miles (161 sq km). Sometimes just one echoing roar will send predators running in the opposite direction, and other times it's a fight to the death. Even though male lions are strong, it's actually the females that do most of the heavy lifting. While the males are busy on guard, females raise the cubs and do all the hunting. And you wouldn't want to be staring down a pride of these frisky felines come mealtime—there's a good chance you'd be on the menu!

STUMP
YOUR PARENTS

Have your parents take the lion quiz below.
If you know more answers than they do,
you'll have a *purrr-fect* excuse to brag.

ANSWERS ON PAGE 43

1 Where do lions live?
A. Africa and Asia
B. South America and Asia
C. North America and Africa
D. South America and North America

2 What is the hair around a male lion's face called?
A. A mullet
B. Feathers
C. A mane
D. A moustache

3 Who are the primary hunters?
A. Male lions
B. Lionesses, or female lions
C. Lion cubs
D. They share the hunting responsibility

4 What do lions eat?
A. Antelopes
B. Zebras
C. Wildebeest
D. All of the above

5 Lions are excellent _____.
A. Runners
B. Swimmers
C. Dancers
D. Climbers

6 Lions are the only cats that live in groups called
A. Herds
B. Prides
C. Flocks
D. Packs

7 A male lion's roar can sometimes be heard how many miles (km) away?
A. 1 (1.6 km)
B. 3 (5 km)
C. 5 (8 km)
D. 10 (16 km)

8 A typical meal for an adult lion is 15 pounds (7 kg) of meat, though lions can eat as many as ___ pounds in a sitting.
A. 30 (14 kg)
B. 40 (18 kg)
C. 50 (23 kg)
D. 60 (27 kg)

9 Male lions stay with a pride for how long?
A. 2 to 4 years
B. 5 to 7 years
C. 8 to 10 years
D. A lifetime

10 What habitat do lions live in?
A. Grasslands and plains
B. Rain forests
C. Marshlands
D. Jungles

Lion cubs are born with brown spots.

The lion's habitat once spanned from Greece through the Middle East into Northern India.

Male lions that live in hot, dry habitats have smaller manes than those that live in cooler places.

A small number of white lions live in South Africa.

Sea turTle

If there were an ocean Olympics, sea turtles would definitely get a medal in swimming. These long-distance marathoners spend their entire lives traveling the ocean to find food and a mate. And they have a great sense of direction. Female sea turtles return to the beaches where they were born to nest and lay eggs. For one loggerhead sea turtle, that meant a 9,000-mile (14,484-km) journey across the Pacific Ocean! Leatherback sea turtles often travel 3,000 miles (4,828 km) or more to return to their nesting beaches. Scientists still don't completely understand how turtles know exactly where to go to lay their eggs. Maybe they stop at a "Shell" station to ask for directions!

Double Take

See if you can spot 10 differences in the two pictures.   ANSWERS ON PAGE 43

A green sea turtle and fish swim on the Great Barrier Reef in the South Pacific Ocean, Australia.

ed or endangered.

Leatherback sea turtles can weigh more than a ton (2,000 lbs/907 kg).

...and sea turtles survives to adulthood.

Sea turtles once shared the Earth with dinosaurs.

NATIONAL GEOGRAPHIC
KIDS™

NATIONAL
GEOGRAPHIC

Some sea turtles build decoy nests to trick predators.   **All sea turtle species are threaten**

Sea turtles can expel excess salt through glands near their eyes.   **Only one in every thou**

WoLF

Have you ever been outside at night and heard an eerie, high-pitched howling that sounds a little too close for comfort? Believe it or not, that call you hear belongs to none other than man's best friend—well—kind of. Wolves are the largest members of the dog family and ancestors of your pet Fido. They are widely spread all over the world and can be found in places like the forests of Germany, the tundras of Russia, the mountains of Tibet, and the deserts of Israel—just to name a few. And that howl you hear? It's not meant to scare you, though it could possibly tell a potential threat to back off! Wolves are very social creatures that live and hunt in packs. Communication is very important. Besides howling, they also whimper, whine, growl, bark, yelp, and snarl—that's how they stay in touch.

STUMP
YOUR PARENTS

If your parents can't answer these questions about wolves, maybe they should go to school instead of you!

ANSWERS ON PAGE 43

① In what type of environment do wolves typically live?
A. Desert
B. Rain forest
C. Savanna
D. Forest

② Wolves communicate by
_____.
A. Chirping
B. Squealing
C. Buzzing
D. Howling

③ A group of wolves is called _____.
A. A pack
B. A herd
C. A flock
D. A swarm

④ What is a baby wolf called?
A. A cub
B. A calf
C. A pup
D. A foal

⑤ What is the largest species of wolf?
A. Red wolf
B. Gray wolf
C. Italian wolf
D. Werewolf

⑥ How many wolves generally live in one group?
A. 2 to 5
B. 6 to 10
C. 8 to 18
D. 10 to 24

⑦ Wolves are known for which strong body part?
A. Their jaw
B. Their hind legs
C. Their paws
D. Their tail

⑧ What is the main threat to the wolf population?
A. Hunters
B. Asteroids
C. Loss of habitat
D. Pollution

⑨ What do wolves generally eat?
A. Hamburgers and french fries
B. Grasses and rodents
C. Deer and elk
D. Other wolves

⑩ If you were a wolf, how would you walk?
A. Standing upright
B. On all fours, flat-footed
C. On all fours, on just the tips of your toes
D. You could either walk on all fours or standing upright

...es are also members of the dog family.

...at mostly large hoofed animals, including moose and bison.

Some ancient cultures worshipped wolves as gods.

Wolves almost never attack humans.

NATIONAL GEOGRAPHIC
KIDS™

Ethiopian wolves have appeared on national stamps.

One wolf can eat 20 pounds (9 kg) of food at a time—That's about 80 hamburgers!

Like the wolf, foxes, jackals, and coy

Gray wolves

penGuiN

What's black and white and never in flight?
If you guessed penguin, you're right! Unlike most of our feathered friends, penguins lost the ability to fly a few million years ago. In fact, their wings have turned into paddle-like flippers just perfect for swimming. Their bodies are made for the water. They even have down underneath their dense feathers that acts like a waterproof bodysuit. The feathers keep the penguins warm and streamlined so they can effortlessly glide through the water looking for a tasty meal of fish. Most penguins need to be warm and toasty since they live and swim in cold waters, particularly in the polar regions of Antarctica. But there is one species that lives as far north as the Galapagos Islands. To beat the hot equatorial temperatures, Galapagos penguins give off excess body heat through their flippers and feet—and sometimes pant like dogs!

Funny FILL-IN

Penguin Paradise

Ask someone to give you words to fill in the blanks in this story without showing it to him or her. Then read it out loud for a laugh.

Today _____ and I went to the aquarium. We saw all kinds of
       best friend's name

_____ and _____ , but I liked the penguin exhibit
  marine animal plural   *marine animal plural*

most. They were so _____ when they _____ . The trainers
           adjective   *verb past tense*

were inside the habitat feeding them _____ and asking the audience
                       food

questions. Did you know there are _____ different species? If someone in the audience
                  number

got the answer right, they got to _____ the penguins a (n) _____ .
                  verb   *food*

One penguin was so _____ , it _____ in
          adjective   *verb past tense*

the _____ and did _____ _____ .
    liquid   *number*   *noun plural*

It was the _____ thing I've ever seen!
     adjective ending in -est

Penguins and polar bears never meet in the wild because they live at opposite poles.   **Emperor p**

Some African penguins have fallen prey to leopards.   **French explorer Dumont d'Urville nar**

...nguins sometimes adopt orphaned chicks.

...ed Adélie penguins after his wife.

Adélie penguins steal pebbles from each other's nests.

Male emperor penguins balance their eggs on their feet.

KOALa

If you're ever in Australia, you might look up into a eucalyptus tree and spy a gray ball of fur clinging to a branch. If you think it's a koala bear, you're only half right! Koalas actually aren't bears at all—they're marsupials. Just like their kangaroo cousins, koalas are born before they're fully developed, and crawl into a pouch on their mother's belly to finish growing up. Newborn koalas, called joeys, are blind, deaf, and only about the size of a jelly bean! As adults, koalas spend their days eating the juicy tips of eucalyptus leaves. These leafy greens are poisonous to most other animals, but koalas have special bacteria in their stomachs that prevent them from getting a bellyache. Yum!

39

Funny FiLL-IN
Koala Hunt

Ask someone to give you words to fill in the blanks in this story without showing it to him or her. Then read it out loud for a laugh.

I just got back from the most _____ trip to Australia with
                                      adjective

my _____ . We went _____ in a
        relative   verb ending in –ing

forest full of eucalyptus trees because I was _____
                                                   verb ending in –ing

to see some koalas. It was _____ and _____
                                  adjective   adjective

outside, and after two _____ of searching, all we had seen
                            units of time

was a (n) _____ and a couple of _____ .
               animal   different animal plural

Suddenly, I heard a (n) _____ coming from somewhere
                            animal sound

above me. I looked up and sure enough there were _____ koalas
                                                        number

sitting in one tree! " _____ !" My cousin yelled.
                            exclamation

"They're so _____ !" I wanted to take one home with me,
                 adjective

but I didn't think it would be allowed on the _____ .
                                                  mode of transportation

Luckily, I had my camera, so we took lots and lots of _____ .
                                                            noun plural